canal
SEASONS

Clive Doucet

 Penumbra Press
Poetry Series #53

Copyright © Clive Doucet and Penumbra Press, 2003
Published by PENUMBRA PRESS
Printed and bound in Canada. Cover art by Tammy d'Entremont.
No part of this publication may be reproduced, stored in a retrieval system or transmitted, in any form or by any means, without the prior written consent of the publisher or a licence from The Canadian Copyright Licensing Agency (Access Copyright). For an Access Copyright licence, call toll free to
1-800-893-5777 or visit www.accesscopyright.ca

NATIONAL LIBRARY OF CANADA CATALOGUING IN PUBLICATION

Doucet, Clive, 1946-
    Canal seasons / Clive Doucet. — 1st ed.
(Penumbra Press poetry series ; 53)
Poems.
ISBN 1-894131-43-6
    1. Ottawa (Ont.)--Poetry. 2. Seasons--Poetry. I. Title. II. Series.
PS8557.O787C35 2003   C811'.54   C2003-905330-X

Penumbra Press gratefully acknowledges the Canada Council for the Arts and the Ontario Arts Council for supporting its publishing programme. The publisher further acknowledges the financial support of the Government of Canada through the Book Publishing Industry Development Program (BPIDP) for our publishing activities. We also acknowledge the Government of Ontario through the Ontario Media Development Corporation's Ontario Book Initiative.

To Emma who followed me
down to the water

and

David Kealey who founded
the Bytown Boat Club

CONTENTS

PROLOGUE
    Ottawa, 10
    Poets and Boats, 13

SPRING

    Morning on the Water, 21
    Seasons, 22
    Spring Scent, 23
    Rites of Spring, 24
    Geese Going North, 26
    So the Water is Back, 27
    Morning Angels, 28
    Friends, 29
    Poisson d'avril, 30
    Sail, 31
    Dippered, 32
    Life and Lifestyle, 33
    Mister Loon, 34
    Weasels, 35
    To my Daughter, 36
    Through the Shadows, 37
    Encumbered, 43
    Money, 44
    Magnificent, 45
    Meditations by Bank Street Bridge, 47

Junk, 48
The Duck Club, 49

SUMMER

Bring on the Lions, 53
Rainbows, 54
Angels, 55
Disappearing, 56
Wake, 57
Dow's Lake Marsh, 58
A Single Affaire, 60
Row, 61
Clouds, 62
Ode to a Rainy Morning on the River, 64
Fizzy Fish, 66
Vanishing, 67
Bank Street Bridge, 68
Here, 69
Comfort, 70
Blue and Heron, 71
Cousin, 72
The Rowing Gull, 73
Poets, 74
A Race, 78
Reflections by Bank Street Bridge, 79
Ducks, 81
An Old Bytown Drinking Song, 82
Seagulls, 83
Brick Chains, 84
Of the Progress of the Soul, 86

Late in the Season, 87
Ease, 88
Ducks, 89
Winners, 90
Instant, 91
Duomos, 92
August Gold, 93
Bloom, 94
Apologies to Arkansas, 95
Nails, 96

FALL

Leaves on the Water, 99
Some Days, 100
Reflections by Bank Street Bridge, 101
Requiem, 102
A Horse of a Different Colour, 105
Head of the Rideau, 107
Giddy, 108
Last Day on the Water, 109
Putting up Boats for Winter, 110
Marsh Loosestrife, 112
Robin, 113
November, 114
Tipped, 115

WINTER

Rowing Ice, 119
First Snow, 120

Edge, 121
Catch the Sun, 122
Between Fifth and Bank Streets, 123
Altar Boys, 125
Snowflakes, 129
Orion, 130
Christmas Star, 131
Winter Sparrows, 132
On Meeting a Friend, 133
Unboated, 134
The Lady of Lac Dow, 135
Ondes Lumineux, 138
En Baudelaire, 139
Reflections by Bank Street Bridge, 142
Cycles, 144
Between Constellations, 146
Hexagons, 147
March Snow, 149
Waiting, 150
Moonstones, 151
Bus Stop, 152
March 20, 153
April Complaint, 155
Stars, 156
Sky, 157
Requited, 158

EPILOGUE

PROLOGUE

OTTAWA

THE CITY OF OTTAWA exists in the imagination of the Inuit as the "place which is always green." In the imagination of Albertans, it is the place where western taxpayers are sacrificed on eastern altars. The Torontois regard Ottawa with the voluptuous disdain of Bay Street and warmer climes for the isolates of Brasilia, north. And in the imagination of the Quebecois, Ottawa is a too comfortable, double bed that they will soon be exchanging for the tranquillity of separate beds.

The reality is a little different. The reality is Ottawa does not exist. For a city to exist, it must first be defined in the language, hearts and imaginations of its own citizens. Ask an Ottawan what he or she thinks of their city and they will tell you about skiing in the Gatineau Hills or skating on the canal. They will also tell you that it is a great place to bring up children and converse with your neighbour. It is all these things. But a city to be a city must be more than a site for activities. It must develop a soul which is inalienably its own. This is the destiny of all great cities, be they Paris or St. John's, Newfoundland.

Ottawa is not a city, but it has been a summer campsite for aboriginal people for millennia. Perhaps, that is why aboriginal people tend to feel comfortable here. It was their campsite at the juncture of three rivers and the taste of that original occupation still lingers. It still feels like a good place to camp. Wild animals have not been exiled to some distant place. Wolves still roam a few miles from Parliament Hill. Bears still come down from the hills to roam in gardens. The boreal forest still laps at the edges of the rivers reminding the present inhabitants that the earth is a large place and people are small.

The Parliament Buildings have a majestic presence at any time of the year. They are etched serenely along a cliff top above the broad river, but the streets and buildings, which border these imposing structures have never coalesced into a resonating partner. Instead Ottawa remains a collection of little urban campsites with names like the Glebe, Lower Town and Sandy Hill bivouacked along the rivers, each having little connection to the next.

The people in the campsites live without great interest in the notion that they reside in the nation's capital. Native Ottawans go about their days, busy with their own gardens, streets and small concerns invisible to visitors and visiting politicians. This invisible clothing is essential in order to keep the national dyspepsias away from their own hearths which regularly sweep across the nation and come to focus uneasily on Parliament Hill.

The invisibility of the natives is one of the reasons visitors often remark Ottawa is a pleasant but dull city. It is dull because the residents have long learned to bivouac, far away from the inspecting eyes of journalists and visitors alike. But wearing protective clothing is not the stuff of the agora, of the vibrant public voice on which every city depends to define itself. It is the stuff of private lives.

In short, do not expect a city when you visit my village, it hasn't got there yet. Instead expect a northern place where the dramas of the seasons play themselves out fiercely. Ottawa does not have a temperate, European climate meandering gently from a cloudy, damp winter to a long, mild summer. It is the coldest capital on the planet, colder than Moscow, colder than Stockholm. There is no mistaking winter in Ottawa. It introduces itself with a crack of driving snow in November and the cold remains soldered to the ground for five months of dark nights, icy waterways, and leafless trees cut with frost.

Spring comes after this long, fierce hibernation at first so hesitantly that the inhabitants begin to fear that this will be the year that summer will forget them. Then suddenly, God snaps her fingers and spring arrives with such a burst of bubbling happiness that its strength never fails to astonish and delight. The crocuses push through the snow like cosmic magic with the tall tulips following, flaring with such neon colour after the long white months of winter they appear too bold to be believed.

Best of all spring is the harbinger of a tropical summer. A time when the ice scars are bathed away by long hot days, bathtub nights and the earth explodes with new leaf and wing until every village creaks joyously with life. Until, autumn slowly, solemnly begins to interject with cooler nights, changing colours, building slowly towards its brilliant crescendo.

For those who grow up in this northern village, these great seasons become imprinted on the soul while the village itself becomes both a refuge from and courtier of this annual round.

POETS AND BOATS

EXPLAINING A PASSION for rowing to someone who has never felt the exhilaration of moving a pencil thin skiff quickly over the water is an improbable task. Among Canadians, the subject often sparks incomprehension, such as "do you mean canoeing?" Or a kind of smug comment on social class, such as "oh yes, like the boat race on the Thames, Oxford-Cambridge." Of the two reactions, I prefer the first. At least, it isn't confused with any facts. The reality is rowing in Canada has always been the sport of ordinary people who develop an unreasonable and unmaterial love of an eccentric endeavour. Money has never had much to do with it.

But if I had to explain why people are willing to drive ramshackle cars but buy expensive, impractical boats, I would do it this way. Rowing is the closest thing I know to flying. If you looked down from a plane at a bird flying over the water, you would notice that the graceful rise, fall, and glide of the birds wings are remarkably similar to the motion of a sculler opening and closing the sculls and then gliding across the water. Only the orientation is different. The avian movement is in a vertical plane, the human horizontal but the one motion mimics the other, and as you become skilled at sculling, it begins to feel as if you are flying, balanced on the cusp, between the two great mediums of the planet, water and air. The exhilaration is both complex and primitive. At racing speed, it's a pure adrenalin rush. More slowly, it's metaphorical and meditative.

It is, nonetheless, an eccentric sport especially in

Canada where Canadians should be disadvantaged by climate but have proved to be among the best in the world. I take mischievous delight in the improbable symmetry that the 20th century has been bracketed for Canada by two great world champions — Ned Hanlan at the beginning, Silken Laumen at the end. Mischievous because it should never have happened, for Canada is not a logical place for great scullers to evolve, delighted because it did happen. One was a man, the other a woman, both extraordinary.

Oarsmen and women practice for a race in pieces and by seasons. The winter is reserved for the long, slow, slog of strength and stamina conditioning, autumn for the head race festivals, summer for the adrenalin of sprint races and spring for delight. A sculler rarely races a full 2,000 metres in practice. This kind of all-out effort is reserved for the exhilaration and pain of the race day. What the athlete does in practice is to go for long, stamina building rows or selects a small piece of the stroke cycle and focuses on perfecting it.

It is like practising a piano piece where one troublesome section of the tune is rehearsed over and over again. It could be the first three strokes of the race or perhaps perfecting the glide as the sculler returns from the finish position where the blades leave the water to the start position where the blades enter the water again.

The entire motion of the stroke cycle must be perfect because for the boat to fly, it must move continuously and easily forward without any noticeable hesitation at any point, just as a bird flies in the air without any check. Any imbalance or imprecision slows or tips the boat. It is not enough to simply be strong. Elegance of motion is required for speed as well as beauty.

The closest thing to a rowing coach is a ballet master where the same psychology of perfection and continuing critique of fundamental elements are required to form an elite dancer.

Beyond the race, the discipline of rowing becomes, as with the practice of dance or music, part of a life discipline that transcends any single performance into a metaphor through which one's life is felt and expressed. By this measure, winning or losing a race is irrelevant. By this measure, the experience of the sculler is defined exclusively in unique, personal terms — what each person brings to the sport and takes away from it.

It is an intense and singular experience which when combined with the adrenalin of competition can quickly evolve into a bond that can consume a lifetime. The self-absorption at the Olympic level is awesome as athletes and coaches disappear into the early morning and the mantra of race preparation.

As a young man, the self absorption of racing both fascinated and repelled me. My own confusions led me into disagreements with coaches, and a racing career of little consequence. But through all the sound and fury, of both loving and hating the drudgery of race training, my affection for the sport never dimmed. There was something utterly, engaging about the sport that captured me from the first instant. Only human beings could have invented something so odd, so impractically combining crude muscle with great delicacy of execution.

And I have always loved the early quiet of the first light

upon the water, when oarsmen are obliged to practice. There is an ethereal quality to watching the world wake up as you ease silently through the membrane of a new day that is like no other experience.

These poems were written during the time David Kealey was putting together the Bytown Boat Club. It was a small neighbourhood club which used the Rideau Canal and the little lake that sits like a teaspoon between the Experimental Farm and the Glebe. No doubt, a boat club devoted to the rowing and literary arts seems a childish thing for grown men and women to occupy themselves with. It earned no money, created no visible profit, but there are things of great value in life that don't carry price tags or easy visibility.

The poems are divided into the seasons and together form a suite following the seasonal round. They come also from my friendship with David Kealey and the people who joined him to form the Bytown Boat Club. David was clearly the best and most knowledgeable sculler among us and in another club would have been regarded as the Director and Principal Coach, instead he took the title of Chief Gardener. His principal responsibilities were to coach and plant flowers, treating the small place where we launched the boats from the edge of the lake like a garden. He had two graceful, old sculls that he had inherited from a lifetime of racing. Determined to make a success of the club, he began coaching full-time, teaching children and adults, some for a fee, many for free.

Being a poet, it seemed natural that I should become the Club's Resident Poet and I set about writing a poem, then hammered it up on a post by the boat rack. The first one I wrote begins this collection. I had never felt the slightest inclination to do anything like this before and have rarely read my work in public. Yet, I found this a rather natural and satisfying thing to do — to tack a poem up for passers by.

One evening, I came unexpectedly upon one of my companions reading a poem that I had written and pinned up. Concentrating on the little sheet of white paper, he didn't see me and it seemed to me that this was the way it was supposed to be. Poetry shouldn't be locked up in thin books in appropriately literary bookstores. Poetry should be out there, in the community, part of people's lives. And it could be, that's what nailing a poem to a plywood board by the edge of the lake said to me. It was an enormously important discovery for me. In my imagination, I understood how Martin Luther must have felt nailing his articles to the church door. It had the liberating feeling of once and for all declaring yourself.

Our first Club Regatta was called the Poets-in-Boats Regatta. It was meant to be a Festival in the old Athenian ideal of celebrating mind, body and spirit. We invited eight women artists to exhibit their works on the shore and called them "The Women's Eight Art Show." All athletes and poets were required to read at least one poem from a sailboat tethered from the dock. Prizes were awarded to the best times on the water and the best poems from the sailboat. Instead of a medal as prize, the award was something called a poem box, a little paper box that inside held a poem and could be hung around the neck with a piece of ribbon as if it were a medal.

The philosophy of the Regatta was to create an event in which the connections between the athletic arts, the visual and literary arts could be celebrated together in a single festival which honoured the human spirit, mind, and body.

The connections between a garden, reading poetry and a boat club may seem incongruous, but they have more in common than is first apparent. Gardens give the children the illusion of adventurous spaces all the while being safely fenced off from the wider world and the hurts it may bring. The safety of the garden is an illusion because children must grow up to suffer the discipline of work and the indignities of life. But while they last, gardens are a wonderful thing, not only for the happy times that they afford, but ever after in memory when "in despair with fortune and men's eyes," a summer evening beside the lake, a boat moving silently over the water, the quiet voices of friends return to warm the coldest, hardest day.

SPRING

MORNING ON THE WATER

There is a celestial order
which floats
in still cobwebs
above clear water.
It is as timeless
as mountain tops,
as splendid
as spring flowers.
It weaves
in evanescent nets
disappearing with the sun.
Forgotten
for another day
the mortality of moments
the infinity of days.

SEASONS

There is a season
for tourists
and time for locals.
In Ottawa,
the season is spring
and the time is cold
when like an old, mangy dog
winter grudgingly retreats
down cold, watery lane ways
leaving grey snow fingers
upon the streets.
And the locals,
bleary eyed
emerge from huts
to shake themselves
and wonder at the scent
of another season.

SPRING SCENT

Ottawans stoop towards spring
like starving hawks
towards slow, soft bellied prey.

RITES OF SPRING

The local rites
are held at Skyline
on the little mountain
where the snow holds
in small winter glaciers.
Here, in the belly of spring,
young monsieurdames
gather like large eared elephants
in the dusty, African heat.
At Skyline, they roll and roil
in the snow scalded sun,
locked in a daze
of valium joy;
beer splashed
on sweating sides,
skin burning,
while the ski runs
mound into sugar hills
and strange, brown spots
begin to sprout on the flats
in greetings
from a different world.

The old men
remember
when they were young
and laughed at mortality,
feeling nothing,
but the echo of their own eternity;

feeling the world turning
from snowfield
to hill grass;
feeling the echo of a young woman
who rises to meet the day
exactly as they do
with burning shivers
from foot to groin to brain.

Skyline
is the place
our elephants
come to be born.
It is the place
young Ottawans
discover they are young,
and lumber happily after each other;
while the spring sun
fries the white snow hills
with shades
of Gstaad.

GEESE GOING NORTH

Each year,
they fly
across the sky,
exultant,
noisy,
phoenix
rising from the ashes
of another winter
towing the summer
towards us.
Poems at their wing tips,
harsh voiced,
strong,
impervious
to my admiration.
A blessing on my eyes.
God's fingerprints
in the sky.

SO THE WATER IS BACK

So the water is back
and spring has begun
with water boiling
through the locks.
We uncover the boats
and begin to paint,
and shellac,
and oil.
It is a restless feeling.
A feeling of another year,
another growing season,
of flowers at the throat,
the moribund hand of winter
finally slacked
and hacked away.
A great, dark, winter carp
jumps
slapping the surface
of the water
with a crack.
He seems unaccountably fat,
an improbable creature
to have lived
buried beneath
the freeze.
Improbable as I,
standing nervously
on the shore.
Will I be an oarsman again?
Will I have survived?

MORNING ANGELS

In the morning,
there are angels
that come to rest
on my fingertips.

There are angels
which come to sing
me songs and whisper
tales of sunlit days.

I have felt them flutter
around me
with the ease of old campaigners.

I have felt their laughter
at my awkward movements.

They are not magical.
They are just there
waiting to be heard,
waiting to be seen,
waiting to hold today
and sustain tomorrow.

FRIENDS

Befriending a carp
is not an easy thing.
They are not princes
of anything,
but murky, muddy depths
with fat snouts and curving bellies.
They ease about your boat,
wet dinosaurs
ready to serve lunch
and be served.

POISSON D'AVRIL

Newfoundland
has changed place
with Bermuda.
This has caused
confusion for the tourists
who want their money back,
and for the Bermudians
who shiver in their shorts.
The Newfies are hot,
but adapting.
And in Ottawa,
snowflakes have changed
to Belgian chocolates,
cars into snowflakes,
politicians into lumpen proletariat.
And if you believe all this
then here is a kiss,
given April 1, 1993.

SAIL

We are all sailing somewhere.
That is why people
like to mess about in boats,
a boat is a metaphor
for another journey
felt but not seen,
that eagles about the edges of life.

DIPPERED

In the May sky,
Ursa Major
sits above
our house
like a starry cap.
We sit outside
floating about inside
the square of stars:
Juno, the Goddess;
Jasmin, the poet;
Huard, the loon;
Paris, the lover;
Melaneus, the murderer;
Clive, the oarsman,
Julian, the actor,
Patty, the thinker,
Days past, present and future.
People past, present and future.
What a tangle spring is.

LIFE AND LIFESTYLE

A lifestyle has things.
A life has people,
community and purpose.

MISTER LOON

Mister Loon
comes sweeping
over the water.
Fat, mysterious Mister Loon,
with his white tie necklace,
sails just above my head.
Content, he is a gentleman,
and I — helpless to disturb him.
My narrow skiff
and long oars
ridiculous
as the Great Blue Heron
who promenades with antique motion
in the reedy shallows,
long beaked, longer necked,
narrow headed,
his eyes glassy
with perpetual suspicion.
Heron keeps his distance.
Mister Loon
lands in a flurry
near his nest.
It's business as usual,
leaving me and the Heron
to our own strange days.

WEASELS

Weasels are not the most social
of animals.
They slip through the long grass
by the boat house,
skinny,
elegant,
hunting,
blink and they're gone.
They care little
for poetry
and a lot for ducks.

Is the weasel happy?
is the American question.

Is the weasel's soul saved?
The Catholic question.

Where was the weasel
when paradise was lost?
Is the poet's question.

And the weasel?
Well, the weasel cares little for poetry
and a lot for ducks.

TO MY DAUGHTER
ON HER 18TH BIRTHDAY

Happy birthday
smiling one.
Happy rebellion,
may you smoke dangerously,
drink in moderation,
and cause yourself
the necessary pain
to pass through
the wall of childhood
into my land.
This place,
where people
live like startled deer;
beautiful and gracious,
but always flexed
against the dangers
which inevitably come;
where the world is both grander
and meaner;
where smiles and tears
are never quite so simple;
where trust and truth
are hard fought things;
where fathers are a little smaller
and daughters a little taller.

THROUGH THE SHADOWS

I cannot see
the dapples on the water
without thinking
of Van Gogh.
He caught the essence
of life
more than any other.
He understood it from the inside,
that is why all painting is divided
into before and after Van Gogh;
and why biographers stare in at him
from the outside
like jailers at a prisoner,
explaining in tome after tome.

It is the man's courage
which is astonishing.
He flamed incandescent
burning at the seeds
of existence.
He did not turn away from the battle.
He stood his ground
until the very end
asking for no mercy.

"In my work,
I risk my life," he wrote
in his last letter to his brother Théo.
"I risk my life."

He knew what he was doing
only the destination eluded.

Dapples of shade
on the water
all day long.
In the late morning,
they are fat and round
like hand prints,
like something
Manet or Monet
would have painted.
And by noon, they are hard and sharp,
but always there,
the light playing tricks
with shadow and space;
the light playing tricks with me.

"You know (Théo)
that one of my principles,
one of the fundamental verities,
not simply of the Gospel,
but of the entire Bible
is the light shining in the shadows,
by the shadows to the light."

And he did struggle
all his life
in the shadows
to move to the light.
The more difficult the journey,

the harder his life,
the more brilliant,
the more colourful,
the more light filled
his tableaux became;
until they were raw with life,
raw with more than we see.
It was as if they were eating him,
and we have been
dining off them ever since.

The Dutchman,
they called him at Arles.
The Dutchman
yet he wrote in French elegantly, powerfully.
Some colleagues at work
call me jestingly un faux Canadien-français,
un faux.
Un faux.
Why?
Because I speak French with an accent?
Because I am not pur-laine?
Who defines who I am?
Where is the measure made?
Louis Riel called himself Métis.
He was only one eighth Indian,
but it was enough to hang him.
And fifty per cent Acadien
makes me un faux.
So be it.
It doesn't much matter.

I define myself in the Dutchman's terms.
From the inside.
The Dutchman.
        The Dutchman.

Sweet Jesus, Vincent,
I sit here looking at the light
on the water
and the dapples crack
with your obsession.
"Le disque solaire,"
comme Aumier a dit.
But it was more than an obsession
with the sun and its sunflower echos.
It was an obsession
with the substance of life.
Monet and Manet's paintings were pretty.
Yours reek with the mystery
of someone who has stuck
his fingers through the interstices
of life in our little envelope.
Like Einstein,
you saw further
than the rest of us,
and in doing so,
pushed at the boundaries
of our existence.
You were an angel,
a crazy angel,
an angel who bit at his fingers
and hacked at his ear.

Yet, you needed no blazon.
You understood life
was more profound
than a Dutchman,
than a faux French-Canadian.
It had something to do
with the way the sunlight
broke on your palette,
broke on the wheat field,
broke inside you
in an unrelenting, eternal echo
which calls
all living things;
which makes us more than merchants of men.

Poor, old Paul Gauguin,
he never understood,
he was so busy trying
to be his own biographer
that genius passed him by
as close as fingertips
against his own cheek,
only in his dying
did he begin to understand
what his friend, the Dutchman
had meant.

"It is a green of a different quality,
of the same value,
in the manner of forming a perfect green
which is made by its vibration,

think of the gentle sound of stems
swaying in the breeze;
it's not convenient at all
as colouring."

You were inside, Vincent.
Inside.
Inside what?
Sweet Jesus,
God-damn, fucking dapples,
leave me alone.
Let me die, stupid.
Let me extinguish myself
like another nameless, shooting star,
like the Dutchman, drowning and
reaching for eternity.

ENCUMBERED

God's grace
descended on me this day.
How wonderful it was
to have Mozartian melodies
at my fingertips
and wings on my soul,
and happiness at my feet.
Encumbered with joy.

MONEY

Will money
float your boat?

Will money
imagine
kingdoms
of delight?

Money is just hamburgers
dressed up.

MAGNIFICENT

At the end of the canal,
a magnificent flight of locks
rises from the Ottawa River.
That's how Colonel By's locks
are always described
in the tourist pamphlets.
In some places,
they're called
Thomas McKay's
magnificent flight of locks
as he was the contractor
who hewed the stone
for Colonel By
to make the
magnificent flight of locks.
Now a magnificent flight of geese
I can see,
there they are
up in the sky honking
their way north.
You can't miss the geese.
Every spring,
they wing northwards
over the city
in great jagged Vs.
Rain or shine,
snow or warm,
high in the sky,
they fly

and with the fall of leaves
return.
Magnificent is a word
which comes to mind.
Magnificent and flight.
I stare down at the locks
searching for the magnificence.
Useful finally emerges.
Useful and clever.
How about useful a flight of locks?
Or how about just locks?

MEDITATIONS BY BANK STREET BRIDGE

You shall make no idols,
nor graven image,
neither shall ye set up
any image of stone
in your own land
to bow down unto it:

But it seems to me we do.
It seems to me Jerusalem itself
has become one large graven image,
where the streets,
walls,
temples,
churches
have become the image of the eternal,
where the faithlenders
shill before the divinity of stone.

JUNK

There was a Raphael sky
over the lake,
the top of the clouds
back lit into gold,
the bottom dark and melancholy.
If I were a painter,
I'd paint it,
fortunately I'm not,
derivative,
renaissance
junk,
they'd say.

THE DUCK CLUB

Ducks have a men's club,
they gather after supper
by the farm bridge,
iridescent green heads
and white collars
declaring themselves
male and proud.
They ponder around
the surface
of the inlet together
while their little brown mates
are off
nursing
the new sparks
past foxes
and raccoons
leaving the men
at the club
to be ducky.

SUMMER

BRING ON THE LIONS

Bring on the lions.
Let them tear at the water
with their claws.
Let them howl at the moon
with impotent meows.
Bring on the lions.
Let them chase and thunder
at our bows.
Bring on the lions.
Let them growl
and shake their manes
and be bloody
at the fang.

Bring on the lions,
and we will glide on by.

We will glide on by.
Our boats singing on the water.
We will glide on by
balanced between motes of sunlight
in perfect momentum.

RAINBOWS

Rainbows are God's paint
and a poet's fancy.
They unfurl between the toes
in bathtubs,
curve between clouds,
dance in the mist
above Hog's Back Falls.
Catch them quick
and buckle them
against the waist
against the days
when the paint
fades to grey.

ANGELS

I met an angel
the other day.
She was about seven
and selling freshie
on the street corner
for 25, 50, and the very large
for 75 cents.
I bought the very small
for 25 cents.
It was tasty
and the angel said:
"Thank-you so very much."

DISAPPEARING

At river's edge,
young mother duck
cares for her little sparks.
Peeking over tall grass,
eyes sharpened
against dogs, cats,
and rats of all sizes,
she's poised to flee,
and little ones to follow,
clustered tight about her duck tail.
But good mother duck
loses them anyway.
Each day, the little cluster
of lively sparks grows smaller.
There were eleven
making merry company,
then nine,
then seven,
then six,
then five,
then three.
The universe eating itself.
That's what disappearing
sparks say to me.

WAKE

Coffee
on the fantail.
Beer
on the bridge.
Oh,
how I like to sail
moored to a rail.

DOW'S LAKE MARSH

Buttercups and cattails,
muskrats and blackbirds,
marsh grass and ducks,
a marsh is a heady, noisy thing
filled with imponderables
that won't adapt
to anything of us;
that is impertinently
its own thing.
Each creature its own loud boss.
The cranky red-winged blackbird
patrols the borders of the marsh
in charge
of four wives, four nests
and any intruder
who disturbs
his ministry.
Fat, comfortable muskrat
swims in the shallows
splitting mussel shells
like peanuts,
littering the muddy floor
with their silver insides.
Green frog sits peaceably
on a lily pad absorbing the sun,
waiting for a wife
to hove into sight,
composing his thesis
on the division of species.

And the Great Blue Heron
repeats his endless mantra
that is imponderable,
that has nothing and everything
to do with us.
Why is it we like to drain
and bulldoze marshes flat?
They fit.

A SINGLE AFFAIRE

A sculling race
is a single affaire
filled with the solitary terrors
of I against the universe.

ROW

The word government
derives from the Greek
word meaning row.

An antique relation
until one recalls
the Greeks conquered the world
and began to invent the west
with notions of democracy,
equality,
citizenship,
mathematics,
philosophy,
medicine,
art,
theatre;
and machines
like the great triremes
powered by free men
choosing a destination,
then rowing towards it.

CLOUDS

Clouds are wisps
of vapour.
Cold, foggy wisps.
I know this
because I have flown
through them and seen
their clammy threads
at the cabin window.
But from their cousin
water,
clouds appear charged
with comfort.
Reminders of life on earth.
In my imagination,
they carry along
Cassandra
who was beautiful,
courageous,
and only at the end gave into
her fate,
fucked Agamemnon
and died — screaming
at the nonsense
of fidelity,
infidelity,
and common sense.

Clouds carry along
across the sky

the cries of Trojan women
and their Greek, 1950's men,
Achilles and company,
secure in the male feeling
that boys must be good, old boys,
who whenever they can
get it up,
and whenever they can't
lament.

Clouds bucket
across the sky
like wild horses,
like coarse, unmade beds.
They are not as they seem.

They are gutted of introspection.
Yet if they hold not
the tangled souls of Cassandra
and Melanaeus,
the old poser Reagan
and eclat of Einstein,
where do they be?
Where are these folks?
And
why am I here?
On this life wire,
grateful
and distrusting of clouds.

ODE TO A RAINY MORNING ON THE RIVER

The Inuit call Ottawa
the green place
which in summer it is;
green like the rain forest,
clouds of billowing colour
against the sky,
in shades of green
across the hills
from oak and maple,
pine and sumach.

It is a place
rich in forest life,
rich in water,
rich in the
va et vient
of earth whispers.

The Algonquin call it
the meeting place,
after the rivers
which converge
from north and south
and east
to tumble over rocky scarps.

In summer,
Nature
takes her purse out,

and dumps
the contents
on the meeting place
uncaring, delighting
only in the mighty roars
of her small creatures.

FIZZY FISH

When the world
is too difficult.
When lovers are punctured
with bullets
for being politically incorrect.
When Jerusalem
curls in the sun
like old road kill,
I can't help myself.
I think of fizzy fish.
Fizzy fish
beneath the water.
Fizzy fish
who blow bubbles
and come in different colours.
Fizzy fish
who swim
about my bow
and whisper tales
of peaceful insurrection.
No doubt,
fizzy fish are
politically incorrect.

VANISHING

What happens
if there is no vanishing point?

No vanishing point
in the painting.

No vanishing point
in the sky.

No vanishing point
in me.

What happens if
the reflections are endless
and the depths forever?

What happens if
time is not linear?
Perspective
does not vanish,
and the boundaries of nations
not measured?

        What
                happens?

BANK STREET BRIDGE

In the early morning,
the lights on Bank Street Bridge
shine on
unmindful of the night's passing.
The sun rises.
The disk of moon fades,
and in small echo,
the round lights on the bridge
cluster like little moons,
like the round lights
clustered along the sides
of the Pont Neuf, Paris.
Except, the scene is too bucolic
to be the Pont Neuf.
There's nothing existential
about the Bank Street Bridge.
The sandy arches of the bridge
match the church beside,
brushed with overhanging trees,
it has the feeling
of the deep country
where people abide comfortably
in perfect harmony
with water, tree and leaf,
without the agony of bad taste
and humbled libidos;
as if we Canadians
complete our days
like hobbits in a satisfied daze
of pleasant days.

HERE

Summer's bower
rocks me in her cradle
soft and low.
The basswood
in the garden
perfumes the evening,
its great, spatulate leaves
my Amazon canopy.
The day gives way
to the night reluctantly.
Like the softest words
spoken in love,
the cat heat
of summer
is here.

COMFORT

Two ducks
like to sit
on the bow
of the old, drunk sailboat.
They are safe out there.
A mallard and his wife
in the comfort of
the setting sun.

BLUE AND HERON

The Great Blue Heron
is the loneliest bird
in the world.
It stands
in the shallows
alone,
refusing to be curious,
refusing all company.
It looks like a tree stump,
and then it flies,
rising slowly to the sky.
It's great wings
beating out
another goodbye.

COUSIN

The fragrance
of a summer evening
rises to meet the night,
a bouquet of perfume and life
that if not heaven itself,
must be a cousin.

THE ROWING GULL

The Rowing Gull
is an odd duck.
It likes to paddle backwards
and quack
faster, faster.

POETS

What shall I say,
since faith is dead
and truth away
from you is fled?
> *Thomas Wyatt*
> (1503-1542)

Good and great God, can I not think of thee
But it must straight my melancholy be?
> *Ben Jonson*
> (1572-1637)

All measure, and all language, I should pass,
Should I tell what a miracle she was
> *John Donne*
> (1572-1631)

Gather ye rosebuds
While ye may,
Old time is still a-flying.
> *Robert Herrick*
> (1591-1674)

Fair tree! For thy delightful shade
'Tis just that some return be made;
> *Anne Finch*
> (1661-1720)

Shall the great soul of Newton quit this earth,
To mingle with his stars, and every muse,
Astonished into silence,
> *James Thomson*
> (1700-1748)

A poet's cat, sedate and grave
As poet well could wish to have,
Who was much addicted to inquire
For nooks to which she might retire,
And where, secure as mouse in chink
She might repose, or sit and think.
> *William Cowper*
> (1731-1774)

I am nae poet, in a sense,
But just a rhymer like by chance
An' hae to learning nae pretence,
Yet what the matter
When'er my muse does on me glance
I jingle at her.
> *Robbie Burns*
> (1759-1796)

In Xanadu did Kubla Khan
A stately pleasure dome decree:
Where Alph, the sacred river, ran
Through caverns measureless to man
Down to a sunless sea
> *Samuel Taylor Coleridge*
> (1759-1796)

When the stars threw down their spears
And water'd heaven with their tears,
Did he smile his work to see?
Did he who made the lamb make thee?

Tyger! Tyger! burning bright
In the forests of the night,
What immortal hand or eye,
Dare frame thy fearful symmetry?
   William Blake
   (1757-1827)

And then my heart with pleasure fills
And dances with the daffodils.
   William Wordsworth
   (1770-1850)

I strove with none, for none was worth my strife:
Nature I loved, and next to Nature, Art:
I warm'd both hands before the fire of Life;
It sinks; and I am ready to depart.
   William Savage Landor
   (1775-1864)

Oh why is heaven built so far,
Oh why is earth set so remote?

I cannot reach the nearest star
That hangs afloat.
   Christina Rossetti
   (1830-1894)

I read these old poets
and smile.
We are such little children,
leaving our small prints
upon the page;
then earth enfolds us
one by one.

No matter
that love is lost.

No matter
that the sweet memory
of Almighty Voice
is recalled.

No matter,
but let them stay awhile,
and like children we converse.
>   *Clive Doucet*
>   (1946-

A RACE

A race is a race
like no other thing,
when the stars wink out
and there is only
the sound
of your own heart.

REFLECTIONS BY BANK STREET BRIDGE

A Tintern Abbey,
a bridge,
the trees at the edge,
a smiling bride,
a smiling groom,
a bouquet of jonquils,
a blue sky,
a white cloud,
an old friend,
a game played,
a daughter
in braids
and pinafore,
a son with strawberry hair
and shining eyes,
a wife with freckles
and glints,
the sun light reflected
on the eddies
in different ways
on different days.
A mystery contained.
A day started.
A life begun in sparkles.

The surface of the water
ripples quietly
towards and away from me
uncertain

as if a small stone
has been thrown
upon the water
holding for a moment
reflections of my life.

The boat skims on
to the hard, flat water,
leaving sounds of the ripples,
and the feel of dappled light,

into the steady hiss
of perfect progress.

DUCKS

Ducks are not
all the same.
Some are clever mothers.
Some stupid.
Some indifferent.
Some cautious.
Some bold.
Some fearful.
Some have lustrous chests
which shine in the evening sun.
But in this way
they are all the same.
All ducks are single mothers.
Mister duck having retired
to put his feet up
and be admired.

AN OLD BYTOWN DRINKING SONG

To-night,
we're hanging a moon
in Mooney's Bay.

Yes,
we're hanging a moon
in Mooney's Bay.

You bet,
we're hanging a moon
in Mooney's Bay.

It's simply delightful.
It's simply so ripefull.
Drunk, knee deep in mud
hanging a moon,
under the moon,
in Mooney's Bay.

(Repeat until cooked.)

SEAGULLS

Seagulls
are the truck drivers
of the avian world.
They slash through the air
with singular strength.
Impervious to the
ordinary of the beak species.
If they were motorized,
they'd have 16 wheels.
Robust, tough, amphibious,
seagulls care little for anything,
but their own aerial highways,
and at mid-day,
park alone
in the middle of the lake,
a dark, grey cluster
announcing seagulls
and truck stop.

BRICK CHAINS

There are noisy bricks in the
Bank Street Bridge.
Red bricks
cemented together
in innocuous commonality,
but each alive
to their common destiny,
each one furious,
each one a terrified prisoner
of their own rough, brick carapace.
Each one longing to be

a financier,
or
a ballerina,
or
a deputy minister,
or
a captain of industry,

anything but innocuous commonality
of bridge bricks.

It is an awful thing
to row beneath these brick dungeons:
The cries of the prisoners
so piercing,
so truck horned,
that one day

in a heaving fit of anger
we freed the prisoners and
tore the old bridge down.

The new one
is of simple cement,
curved in six pleasant arches,
without mortar,
without bricks,
without the sound
of rattling chains.

Free, the bridge bricks
retired happily to Younghusband houses
in the Glebe,
where they live yet,
exporting their social lusts
in more commodious surroundings.

OF THE PROGRESS OF THE SOUL

It seems so easy to progress
if one's name is Donne, John.
One's soul
sails on with hard wood keel,
while the body stays behind to fool.
John Donne; Donne, John (1572-1631)
sails on leaving his poems behind
to hang before me
like cathedrals
floating lightly in the sky
enormous, impressive, beautiful.

LATE IN THE SEASON

There is a mother duck
who has produced a little tribe
late in the season.
She promenades about
with seven small ones
safely brought past the fluff
of new born to the third week.
They cavort about with their tiny wings,
a-flap and a long way from flying.
They seem out of time,
innocent of their tardiness
and the season
which declines.
The spring crop are little
different from their mother
and have become large,
sedate and measured,
moving after the elder
with practised ease.
Summer is still at the dock
and the ladies warm in their shorts,
but the evenings shorten
and the humid bloom of summer
so ripe, you can hear it
tumbling into itself.
Will it last long enough
for the young ones to fly?

EASE

What if we had no seasons?
What if each day floated before us
like a perfect summer day.
The sun haloed
by the fluff of field seeds.
The very air resplendent with life.
What if the ease of summer
never ceased?

DUCKS

There is nothing
quite so dead
as a duck.
It floats in the detritus
of the shore's edge,
sans cérémonie,
neck broken
moving gently
up and down
in the wash
of another day's end.

WINNERS

Say there were winners in life.
Say there was a way to cross
the finish line first.
What contest would it be?
What would you win?

INSTANT

Balanced on the water
in a shell
that will tip
the instant you let go
is a rough metaphor for life.

DUOMOS

There is the Duomo in Florence,
St. Peter's in Rome,
St. Paul's in London,
and in Ottawa,
the Cattle Castle;
rising above the canal,
silvered, bell domed
floating
improbably in the air,
dedicated not to heaven
but to the cow,
which walks
about our little planet
on four feet
an innocent bystander
to the rise and fall
of duomos.
I like it
and hope they don't rename it
for some two footed denizen.

AUGUST GOLD

August gold has arrived
and I can't say
I'm pleased.
The line of green trees
cut by a long, flame
of orange and red.
What is it
that separates this tree
from its fellows?
That announces tout de suite
defeat to cooler nights
and shorter days;
that cries red
at first unlatching
of the autumn door.

BLOOM

There is an ominous gathering
in the air.
The birds which arrived
so hesitantly,
redwing males dragging
their feathers across the continent
followed weeks later
by the females.
Finches lighting here and there.
Robins putting on their ringmaster show.
Now, the redwings swarm in the marsh,
the cattails heaving
with colour and flight.
From tree to tree,
the evening song
shatters in the garden
as the warmth of summer
prepares to bloom with their going.

APOLOGIES TO ARKANSAS

The summer sun ripens
the garden grapes
in my backyard
from dot to purple bunch.
And autumn
grackles descend on them
in noisy troops to fatten
before flying south
to harass farmers
in Arkansas.
My apologies to Arkansas.

NAILS

The last nail of summer
and the first of autumn
are the birds
which begin to wheel
about the sky
in testy crowds.
Erratic, flighty,
as if they cannot decide
to turn with or against
the rotating earth.
It is a cranky sign
for us northerners.
Messengers of summer's
goodbye.

FALL

LEAVES ON THE WATER

Leaves on the water,
leaves
that float
and dance
and skid about,
teasing,
ethereal
between sky
and tree.

I stop to pick
one up.
It curls
in my hand,
damp,
the red veins
spreading
like a road map
of the universe.

SOME DAYS

On some days
the Gods paint billboards
along the water way
explaining $e=mc^2$
and electromagnetic cycles.
Gargoyles are carved
on Cathedral roofs.
There are simple truths,
and great loves
etched in hearts,
surrounding me
with invisible boundaries,
waiting to be discovered,
these secrets
cluster
at the edges of the water
garish as billboards
around a hockey rink,
and I row on,
impervious to anything
but the dull roots of my own bones,
knowing only the Gods
are smiling.

REFLECTIONS BY BANK STREET BRIDGE

What if
I really am a fallen angel?

This would account
for my wings which have been
clipped
and cause me to stumble
about on short feet,
and my harp playing
which is not
what it used to be.

What if
I really am a fallen angel?
And used to be comforted
by divine thoughts.

This would account
for the snakes and ladders
I keep building
in my soul.

REQUIEM

All my life
I have been composing requiems.
Peaceful requiems to charm
the fool eruptions of arterial rage
that flows between men and women,
from parents to children,
from nation to nation
like bad weather.
Uncomprehending.
Violent.
Stupid.

Requiems to disarm
the insecurity of wanting to be first
in pride,
in fairness,
in the memories
of injury
and accomplishment.

Requiems for the repose of dead souls.

And sometimes my requiems
have worked.
They have brought
to a small moment,
a small peace
between father and son,
between husband and wife.

And sometimes,
they haven't.

When the screaming
did not stop,
when it echoed forever
into space,
into memory,
into the soul,
never ceasing,
in a silent, ocean swell
crashing
against a raw nerve shore.
Requiems for the repose of dead souls.

All these years,
I have been burying people,
burying people with the right words

because I was afraid
to deal with the angry moments,
when the peace failed,
when the screaming did not stop,
when it echoed forever
into eyes,
into the heart,
never stopping
written over and over again
scratched over and over again
on uncomprehending ears,
on gutted, helpless eyes.

It's those moments
that are the hard part,
when the requiems
crumbled in my hands
like so much sand
and I was alone;
and heard the dull thud
of children being beaten;
and the pulse
of nations destroyed.

Memories
that drive brave men
into monasteries,
and
Indians onto street corners,
and
poets into poems
called Barbara,
and me into
a boat
looking for a sunrise
to redeem
my own battered soul.

A HORSE OF A DIFFERENT COLOUR

There are alphabet blocks
floating on the water.
Fragments that I row through.
Memories that bump up against the boat.
They burst against the bow
like soap bubbles.
The insides
laden with childish feelings
rush out
twisting
the run of the boat.

How is it
that sunny days
can be so complicated?
That such old memories
can still reach out
and cloud the day
with feelings that
shim and shake?

And then a toy horse
comes galloping over the water,
small, teak brown,
ridiculous, loved,
the gift horse scatters
the old blocks into vague atoms
of existence,
before trotting happily off.

And in a kind of miracle,
I am free;
the boat
and me
balanced.

HEAD OF THE RIDEAU, SEPTEMBER 26, 1993

Rain spitting hard and hurting,
the day sunk away
from the cool delight of autumn
into a grey, raking cold.
Stiff, uncertain,
the oarsmen fight
to finish the race,
squinting into the day's end.
Remembering other moments
when the pale sunlight
illuminated the last, great arch of colour
into a shining day
with the sculls
strung along the watercourse
like dust motes
in the autumn light.

GIDDY

The plum of autumn has come.
The trees are luminous now,
shining brighter and brighter
until they hurt the eyes
with their passage.
Dark bones
showing through,
the skeleton tree is not far off,
leaves chasing leaves
in the wind,
swirling,
dancing again,
giddy at their own going.

LAST DAY ON THE WATER

It was cold enough.
Water freezing
in a thin sheen
on the deck.
My hands and feet numb.
But still
I did not
want to go.
I did not
want to say goodbye
for another year.
And tried
to lock
the sweep of the shoreline
and sky
into the inner eye,
so that the balance of boat
and water and me
could fly on
through the white of winter
to another spring.

PUTTING UP BOATS FOR WINTER

It is always cold
and a little melancholy.
Our bodies bundled
up in parkas.
The cathedral summer gone.
The music blunted.
The water grey and forbidding.
The dock cold
where we would sit
in warm, lazy mornings,
the water glistening,
the sun's aboriginal
ease
chasing
soft shadows away,
leaving only
the gentle warmth
of another day
beginning
in the
spinning
of eternity.

The boats stripped
of their rigging
lie in racks
like long, sad logs
waiting,
and we move stiffly,

stumbling clumsily
through
another ritual,
putting the boats up
for winter.

MARSH LOOSESTRIFE

People are like loosestrife,
not without their own beauty,
but set free upon the world,
they choke off other species
with the death grip
of their own virility.

ROBIN

The birds of fall
are fat.
A robin nestles
flat on the garage roof.
Sunning and sleepy,
he's too portly
to stand comfortably.
His chest the same spreading orange
as the leaves.
Head nods. Feathers fluff.
It will be a long,
slow flight south.

NOVEMBER

November is the dreariest month
when the sun
dries up
and the days lump
into dark mornings
and grey afternoons,
and all the world
searches a place
to hide away,
waiting for winter.

TIPPED

The lake hovers
at the edge
of the great freeze.
Trees and reeds stripped
on the shore.
The water naked
of disguise,
a puddle waiting
to crystallise.
Yet the birds,
still gather
to paddle about,
innocuous, busy
terns,
ducks,
loons,
incongruous all.
Feathers puffed
against the cold.
Has no-one told them?
The earth has tipped,
the sun angled away,
the guard of winter come.
God love us,
because ducks don't.

WINTER

ROWING ICE

Oh, oh, oh,
let's go row.
Let's go row
on ice.

Let's put our boats
down on the first thin skin
of the first fall ice.

Oh, oh, oh,
let's go row
on ice
and play
with the memory of summer days.

Oh, oh, oh,
let's go row
and sweep our blades
across impenetrable,
translucent ice.

Oh, oh, oh,
let's be dumb
and go nowhere,
slow.

FIRST SNOW

There's nothing fatter
than the first snow.
It falls slowly
like lush white petals,
decorating
the ground
with a stately imprint
that all is well.
Winter has come
and tossed away
the meanness of November.

EDGE

The cat tails beside the road
are haloed into spun gold.
The old grass leafed
with the setting sun
as colour spills
across the landscape
like Inca gold
shook from the sky.
The ground waits
in neither winter
or autumn, but balanced
exactly on the cusp of two seasons.
From horizon to horizon,
from roadside marsh
to tree and field,
serene, beaten gold
of a sunset sea
ready for the first white
bite of winter.

CATCH THE SUN

Catch the sun,
Dad.
See there it is!
I skate behind my son
and see the light
playing on the ice
in front of us.

Julian skates
towards and through it.
I've got the sun, Dad.
I've got the sun.
And
we skate
into an infinity
of moments,
the sun, the ice,
Julian and I.

BETWEEN FIFTH AND BANK STREETS

Between Fifth and Bank Streets,
there is a Kyrie Eleison sky.
Each winter, I skate beneath
this great colliding of cloud and space.
Alone
at night,
it can sometimes seem
like the peace that passes all understanding.
And
sometimes, it feels
like a tea cosy set down
over a warm tea pot.
And sometimes it defeats me.

In the Ottawa valley,
there is no ocean sky.
The sky is mostly hidden,
thin slices traced
between river hills.
But
between Fifth and Bank
it is different.
There is more of it.
Here, the stars stretch across the cosmos
in their familiar necklace.
Below, fat brick houses,
spired churches,
and stadium
ramp around the canal

in a comforting progression
of human endeavour
proclaiming
we are busy,
we are prosperous,
we are comfortable,
we are safe.

Between Fifth and Bank,
the winter sky exposes itself
calmly, surely,
in an unending,
in an unknowing,
in a serene and infinite smile.
Leaving me to skate
alone on the edge of forever
like a crazy man
crying
Lord Have Mercy On Us.
Lord Have Mercy On Us.
Lord Have Mercy Upon Us.
As if I were some demented Christian
about to be thrown to the lions.

ALTAR BOYS

Snow blew
down the river
raw and cold.

At Lindisfarne,
Saint Cuthbert
looked across the garden
and dreamed of summer days
when the honey bee
flew lazily over the clover.

Yorkshire
can be
a cold place.

Three hundred Spartans
beat the invincible Persians
at Thermopylae.
They held the pass
to the last man.

Lucky days.

Saint Cuthbert
read the confessions
of Saint Augustine
and pondered his own.

In Ottawa, a poet
wrote a poem
about his daughter
chasing butterflies.
He caught her in a net of words,
dark hair flying,
stick thin legs, fast and graceful,
face joyous,
the reflection in his eyes
forever young, forever wondrous.

The Thebans
beat the invincible Spartans
at Leuctra.

Lucky for some.

Norsemen burnt Lindisfarne
to the ground.
Bee Hives, garden, library, cathedral ashed.
The monks rowed away
into the cold North Sea
with St. Cuthbert's bones
and what manuscripts they could save
from the flames.

Snow blew
down the river
raw and cold.

The Roman Legions
beat the invincible Thebans.

At Durham,
they buried Saint Cuthbert
behind the alter
and began to build
the dream of Lindisfarne again.
Bee hives, gardens, library,
another great stone cathedral,
they could not help it.

Alaric torched Rome
and began to graze through the Empire
eating Pax Romana.

And so it goes,
we humans are compelled
to contrive some order
saint, soldier, poet, scientist, nomad.
We want the world to answer to our call.
We want the world controlled,
to be Boss man of Rome,
to be Caesar of the soul,
and if we cannot,
then we declare a goal
and find a Thermopylae:
a victory of blood,
a victory of prayer,
a victory of sensibility,
a victory of money.

Like lions after prey,
like jackals bowing to hyenas,
men search out their victories,
servants of the past,
altar boys to the rituals
of the Gods.

SNOWFLAKES

There is something immensely comforting
in snowflakes
which fall in slow and silent parade.
They remind me the universe is unfolding,
but do it with a shrug
instead of a curse;
as if in other places,
there are also snowflakes;
or if not snowflakes
then an unfolding
with the usual origins,
arrivals,
and departures.

ORION

Orion sprawls across the winter sky
like some celestial flower
arranged to bloom
not in a poet's time,
but in the time of angels.
The starlight so cold, so long away,
that below
the arches of the bridge
are reduced to miniature.
Its little round lights
defying star gloom
like match flares.

CHRISTMAS STAR

Each Christmas is the same,
each different.
As the longest night descends
to mark the beginning
of another winter;
to mark the long snow wait
for spring.
Christmas stars,
do not let me stray far.
Let me rise
like warm yeast bread
to greet the coldest day
content.

WINTER SPARROWS

There is cold and there is minus 30.
Minus 30 is ice life.
Minus 30 crabs machines
into cranky tin.
Pries into buildings
with bullet frost.
Cement, brick and board
are reduced to canvas,
while the heat of hearth fires
flies out faster and faster
towards a ceramic sky,
only to rebound
emptier, whiter, colder
until people hold themselves
like moveable stones,
their breath sucked in,
their muscles from eyeball
to ankle cramped into tucks;
their heads conscious
only of how the cold hurts
and the distance to the next tent.

ON MEETING A FRIEND

Cat ice
is the ice
of sudden friendship.
It lights across the surface
in round, brittle bubbles
that will shatter to reveal
the stronger stuff beneath.
Cat ice comes before the spring
when the sun strengthens
in the sky
and the blessed feeling of warmer days
rises with the morning.

UNBOATED

Winter is the defining season:
From the first snow
which illuminates the trees
in a soft halo
to the stillness of mid-winter
when the houses
are etched against white landscapes;
and the road
a faint pathway
through eternal snowfields.
Winter is the defining season:
The others are just bookends
preparing
and
departing
for
the defining season.

THE LADY OF LAC DOW
CRU 1994

On one side of the lake
there are small castles,
on the other
a hill
clothed in pine and willow,
between the two
a teaspoon lake
and the Lady of Lac Dow,
who rises in cold
and snowy perfection
to weave her winter web.
Princes alone,
she hath no loyal knight
and true.
Skaters sail by her tower
like sprites upon the ice
unknowing that each winter
from her mirrored life
the Lady of Lac Dow
can grant one wish.
One wish
to a true heart,
One wish
to a loyal heart,
One wish
that is the equal
of all the stars.

The Lady of Lac Dow
safe in her tower,
winter's balm
to a tired soul,
she weaves by night and day
a magic web with colours gay
the wishes of men,
the hopes of women,
the mistakes of both.
Three furred women pass her by,
warm and round like well fed puppies.
A young man with the notion
to play Sir Lancelot,
an older one
already serving in Camelot.
And when the moon
is overhead aglow
with the memory
of other days,
come two young lovers
lately wed:
the Lady of Lac Dow
casts her magic web,
it arcs across
the moonlit night
sparkling round about
the lover's heads.

Unknowing, the lovers shiver
in strange delight
to be there together

on the lake,
on this starry night.
Unknowing, they continue
on their way.
Unknowing the earth
turns on its small,
celestial round,
and the night fades
into the day,
into another winter night,
until
the Lady of Lac Dow
disappears into the back
of another spring.
Her silver arms fall away.
Her perfect face decays.
Her tower crumbles
and she sinks down
into the lake's embrace
down to Chateau Laurier,
the broad stream bearing her far away,
leaving her winter scene
of ice sprites and pinpoint stars,
a princess alone,
she hath no loyal knight and true,
the Lady of Lac Dow.
Alone in some foreign place,
she lies graceful and beautiful,
gently blessing the shore.

ONDES LUMINEUX

I am sitting
on a box horse
beneath the Northern Lights.
Star dust
in my hands.
Skates
on my feet.
Part of a cosmic ray.

EN BAUDELAIRE

Baudelaire
Charles (1821-67)
Les fleurs du mal
Les fleurs de la beauté
pauvre homme
comme un prêtre
du center fold
vous êtes obsédé
par le mystèrê
de l'ordre.

De temps en temps,
je vous imagine
m'accompagnant
sur le canal
dans le beau et dur froid d'hiver.

C'est pas vraiment votre style
les femmes
se cachent
en dessous des robes,
en dessous des chandails montagneuse,
en dessous des foulards,
en dessous des mitaines,
en dessous des parkas inuit.
Et partout,
on trouve les moines,
ils vivent à l'interieur
des moments trops vivaces

et méditent dans les trous rondes
qu'on trouve en orange
partout dans la glace.
Dans ma ville,
on s'appelle ces trous rondes
les trous moines
en hommage des hommes
qui se levent de leur habitat
sous marine pour prêcher
la vie sainte.

Les moines ne sont pas beau.
Ils se penchent en préchantle mal sans les fleurs.
Leurs visages cachés dans leur habit,
souvent un bébé phoque dans les bras,
et Brigitte Bardot dans la tête.
Je ne les hais pas,
mais je ne les aime pas non plus.

Par contre,
je vous aime.
Je vous aimes
parce que
je vous trouve
bon compagnon,
malgré le froid
et la glace dure et étrangèrè
vous
sentez la correspondance
entre moi
et Gordie Howe

qui patine
sur une rivière
plus à l'ouest.

Vous êtes
en effet,
en dépit
de vos ténèbres mélancoliques
un homme qui sait
se souffrir heureusement
comme un fleur
qui fait l'odeur
inconsciencement
pour les abeilles.

Je vous aime
mon cher Baudelaire,
alors je vous en prie,
rends-moi visite
sur le canal
dans le beau et dur hiver.

REFLECTIONS BY BANK STREET BRIDGE

What happens
    if we are
        the highest form
            of life in the galaxy?

What happens
    if Sir Bernard Lovell
        is right?
            That in spite of
                all those

millions and millions
    of stars,

the chances
    of cumulative,
        intelligent life-forms
            arising elsewhere
                are negligible?

What happens
    to all those
        despairing poems?

Ripe with bitterness
        that we are less
                than we should be,
                        and more than we ought
                              to be?

What happens to the
        Love Song of J. Alfred Prufrock?

When he finds out
        being etherized upon a table
                is not only demeaning,
                      it's the only kind
                              of diminution available?

CYCLES

It's all in the stroke cycle,
two arms,
two legs,
two feet,
two hands,
one brain,
165 different muscles,
millions of neurons,
synapses, corpuscles
and one boat,
two oars,
and 30 cycles
per minute,
240 per race
ten races per season
ten seasons per career.
Life tied up
in a Jacques Prévert inventaire.

Life tied up
in grandmother, mother and child.
Days tied up
by sunrise and sunsets.
Bodies by breakfast and dinner.
Seasons by
spring and fall.
Earth by the cycle of the sun.

And then there
are those unbearable moments
balanced between the membranes
of water and air
when it's possible
to imagine
slipping though
the cycles,
slipping through
the boundaries
of the universe
to another place.

To the place where the cycles
are explained.

BETWEEN CONSTELLATIONS

A Viking boat
sailed slowly
between the constellations
above the Milky Way.

I saw it
on a winter night,
moving serenely along
the universal isotherms,
freighted
with my dreams.

HEXAGONS

Snowflakes
falling like psalms.
Hexagons
of hydrogen, oxygen
in the shape of lace.
They
appear faithfully in the evening sky,
each one the same,
each one different.

The snowflakes fall
towards the lake
in the mysterious dance
of my life.
Each one spun silently
on the loom of God,
each one mysteriously printed
exactly, two parts hydrogen
one part oxygen,
each one exactly the same,
each one different.
Like a grate fire
in the creak of the universe,
they speak the language of eternity.
They are relentless,
their own
gloria in excelsis Deo,
their own sum.
They are in my blood

like oceans.
They sail down
from the sky,
new minted,
waiting only to be heard
in the song of a thousand, quiet nights.

MARCH SNOW

The snow of March
falls
heavy, full
poignant with consequence.
March snow is the snow
of southern Christmas cards.
Fat, certain, unrelenting
like a curtain
which will not
be lifted except
to descend again.

March snow
has the certainty
of a beautiful woman
who sits alone
in a cafe,
eating exactly what she should,
drinking exactly what she should,
prepared for what she shouldn't.

March snow
has the disdain
of another spring.
Tired and poignant with consequence.

WAITING

There are two winters.
The winter of iron snow crystals
that blow against the house
and the winter which settles
for the long wait inside
like a bear
curling his claws
in sleep,
slumbering
beneath the mountain
waiting for spring,
waiting to be wakened
by warm sunlight
through the trees.

It is the second winter
which is darkest and hardest.
The one which plays
games with time and mood.
The winter which smiles
at long cross word days,
which hears symphonies
which waits
patiently, impatiently
for warm sunlight
through the trees.

MOONSTONES

All the secrets
of the universe
are hidden in moonstones.
They are chipped
from the centre
of beginnings and ends
into celestial pearls
that skip
from planet to planet,
from place to place.
They are forgotten
and remembered
in a luminous trail
between you and me.

When the winter
is too long,
I will bring you
moonstones
in buckets
until the glow
defeats the snow.

BUS STOP, MARCH 14, 1994

Ottawans stand at the bus stop
like two legged buffalo,
their backs humped against the wind,
hoods and collars up,
silent,
standing in line,
chewing their cud,
the brute force
of the universe
howling around;
they wait in ragged clumps
like buffalo
sure of nothing but survival.

MARCH 20

Ver, veris, spring,
vernal, at the beginning of spring.
Aequi, Aequus, equi, equal,
Nox, noctis, night.
The day divided into
12 hours of light
12 hours of night.
Equi and nox.
My life divided into
before birth and after,
into before school days
and after,
into before marriage
and after,
into before work
and after,
into the sky divided
into an infinite checkerboard
of stars
arranged and numbered
from the intersection
of the lines
stretched at the beginning of spring
between our earth and sun.
My life arranged
along a line
between my mother's heartbeat;
each year,
my life divided

a little differently.
The vernal equinox,
the heartbeat of earth,
one year older,
a little further
from the legs
of the beginning place.
The vernal equinox,
the tree ring of earth,
the day of my birth.

April snowstorms
are like bruises on the soul.

APRIL COMPLAINT

A winter too long
that sticks to the soul
in incumbrances of spring.
April and crocuses struggle.
April and people await
the music of a spring day
hungry.
    What do people do
in warm countries
where there is no April complaint?
Where winter does not
hang about muscled with wet snow.

STARS

Stars,
fiery stars,
I found your
beginning point today
in rainbow crystals
on a snowy field.
Sapphires,
emeralds,
rubies,
glints
of coloured light
as if God has scattered
jewels
in bright sparks
across the white snow.
The children and I
gather them up
into a basket
like spring flowers
and then send them
back to the stars.

SKY

If you came from the stars,
across the aeons
of dark and cold,
upon a planet
that was not cold,
that did not burn, that sparkled
in a great and glorious disk
of sea blue and white swirl;
that was bright
like a great jewel,
you might be forgiven
if, for a moment,
you thought
you'd found heaven.

REQUITED

I love this old planet.
I love the days
when morning comes to me
on silver wings
and sunrise opens my eyes
with the gentlest of enquiries.
I love this old planet
and if I could I would
wrap my arms around it
and pull it to my chest
to keep it safe.

EPILOGUE

THERE IS GREAT JOY in movement and I have always been besotted by it. In my part of the world, this means skiing and skating in winter, and rowing and cycling in summer. I have no wings and cannot fly. I can only watch with wonder as the finches careen about my garden surfing on the air waves from tree top to tree branch. But on a sparkling day, when I am cycling across the countryside, the fields and air resplendent, it seems to me as if I am flying; as if I am happy as God intended me to be, in a way that is purely selfish and purely joyful, yet harms no-one; as if I am a small part of some great and happy plan that stretches back through finches and Aristotle to the eternal.

There are different kinds of intelligence. I grew up with a father who was musical, a linguist, a mathematician. I had little of these talents and in a household where the honours were accorded these accomplishments, it was easy to feel stupid. The out-of-doors, the hills and waterways became my escape and later books. Cradled in these places, I grew in my own way, with my own thoughts and in time came to love myself as well as others.

ABOUT THE COVER

The cover and text were designed for the press by Tammy d'Entremont. The photo is of the poet's daughter skimming "on the hard, flat water/leaving sounds of the ripples,/and the feel of dappled light."

The text of the book and the running heads are set in Cartier Book 12/15 at Penumbra Press in Manotick, Ontario.

The Penumbra Press logo was designed by Carl Schaefer, OSA, RCA (1903-1995).